THE
POCKET

Ariana
Grande

Published in 2024
by Gemini Adult Books Ltd
Part of Gemini Books Group

Based in Woodbridge and London

Marine House, Tide Mill Way,
Woodbridge Suffolk, IP12 1AP
United Kingdom
www.geminibooks.com

Text and Design © 2024 Gemini Books Group
Part of the Gemini Pocket series

ISBN 978 1 80247 264 6

A CIP catalogue record for this book is available from the British Library.

Disclaimer: The book is a guidebook purely for information and entertainment purposes only. All trademarks, individual and company names, brand names, registered names, quotations, celebrity names, logos, dialogues and catchphrases used or cited in this book are the property of their respective owners. The publisher does not assume and hereby disclaims any liability to any party for any loss, damage or disruption caused by errors or omissions, whether such errors or omissions result from negligence, accident or any other cause. This book is an unofficial and unauthorized publication by Gemini Adult Books Ltd and has not been licensed, approved, sponsored or endorsed by Ariana Grande or any other person or entity.

Printed in China

Cover illustration by Natalie Floss

10 9 8 7 6 5 4 3 2 1

Images: © Alamy: 7 /David Moffly; 8 /Aflo Co. Ltd. © Getty Images: 4 /Ben A Pruchnie; 28 /C. Flanigan; 64 /NBC; 112 /David Becker.

THE
POCKET

Ariana
Grande

G:

CONTENTS

Introduction

Honesty, openness and engagement are three of Grande's core traits. She is a musician first and foremost, but she is so much more: a style icon, a mentor, a businesswoman and a communicator. Her lyrics touch people around the world, helping them relate to events, emotions and to life. She has suffered, been hurt and learned from the pain. Her fans love her, and she loves her fans. Wise beyond her years, she doesn't even hate the haters, preferring to take the moral high ground, walk away and sing her songs and live her life as she chooses. This is her story...

Chapter One

Early Days

Once Upon a Time...

On 26 June 1993 Ariana Grande-Butera was born in Baton Rouge, Florida. Six months later one of the USA's biggest earthquakes occurred in the San Fernando Valley, Los Angeles. Obviously the two events are in no way related, but Grande's domination of the music scene and her amazing journey to becoming one of the biggest music acts of all time are seismic events. But who is she and how did she start this incredible journey to uber-mega-superstardom?

As Grande admitted, telling
Vogue in 2019:

"My family is eccentric and weird and loud and Italian..."

Italian Family

Grande's early years, until her parents separated when she was around 8 years old, were spent with her mother and father, Joan Grande and Edward Butera, and her half-brother Frankie (her mother's son from a previous relationship), who was a few years older. In a 2018 tweet, Grande famously described herself as "Italian American, half Sicilian and half Abruzzese..." and the close family bonds associated with people from that part of the world (and the New World – Joan is Brooklyn-born) are apparent. She is close to her mother's mother, Marjorie, as well as Joan of course, who frequently accompanies her on interviews.

Her parents apparently
chose her name after being
inspired by Princess Oriana
from the 1989 animated
movie *Felix the Cat*.

Young Ariana

She called the family the
"stereotypical poker-playing, loud,
friendly, food-shoving, loving, Italian
family" in *Complex*, and the bonds
run deep in the Grande family,
particularly the strong matriarch,
and Ariana's mother has had a huge
influence on her.

When describing her mother, she added,

"My mom is a CEO and owns a company that manufactures communications equipment for the Marines and the Navy, so she's not really the housewife type, if you get what I'm saying. She's the most badass, independent woman you'll ever meet – not the cookies-in-the-oven type."

When it comes to her grandmother, however, she was more domestically adept:

"Nonna is the best cook in the world."

Dark Core

Both parents worked – mom as a big boss, dad as a graphic designer – and the family lived very comfortably in a gated community. But there was an ever-present fascination with the darker side of the world: "One year [on Halloween] when I was a little kid she [Joan] smeared blood all over the walls in our new house and said O.J. did it." And as she told *Billboard*, she was "a very weird little girl... Dark and deranged..."

This demonstrates one of the many paradoxes associated with Ariana Grande: beneath the "American Sweetheart" looks is a darker core, one that has experiences of loss and sadness. And according to Ariana, Joan is a goth, with a wardrobe of nothing but black clothing.

Colourful Father

Ariana's father Edward has been less of an influence on her life and work, but that is to be expected as he was not ever-present after her parents' divorce. But given that Edward is a graphic designer, photographer and artist, perhaps some of the more colourful traits of Grande's character are inherited from her father.

Both parents are
mentioned in the lyrics
of her hit song 'Thank U,
Next', which lists many of
her relationships, including
the romantic ones, and the
help they have been to her
in terms of learning and
growing as a person.

Five Fun Facts

1 While her parents chose her name from *Felix the Cat*, ironically, Ariana is allergic to cats. She is also allergic to bananas.

2 As a child, Grande performed with the Fort Lauderdale Children's Theater in the lead role the musical *Annie*.

3 She has 12 dogs. Their names are Strauss, Ophelia, Toulouse, Cinnamon, Coco, Fawkes Kitty, Lafayette, Myron, Snape, Lily, Pignoli and Sirius Black (named after the fictional godfather in the *Harry Potter* series).

4 She is a huge fan of Harry Potter. Her favourite characters are Luna Lovegood and Draco Malfoy. There is also a character named Ariana Dumbledore in the books.

5 Two of her fashion icons are Marilyn Monroe and Audrey Hepburn.

*

Musical Influences

Grande credited Gloria Estefan with inspiring her to pursue a music career after Estefan saw and complimented Grande's performance on a cruise ship when she was 8 years old.

Mariah Carey and Whitney Houston were her main vocal influences, as well as Beyoncé, Celine Dion and Brandy (saying that her "riffs are incredibly on point").

Young Performer

Destined and trained to be a performer from a very young age (even karaoke at home with the family), that famous hockey match was certainly not Ariana's first foray into performance. While still at school she sang with the Florida Sunshine Pops orchestra (she also studied the French horn) and she played in the Fort Lauderdale Children's Theater.

One of her productions was *Annie*, another *The Wizard of Oz* (a recurring theme for her) and she tried out for – and scored a part in – the Broadway show *13: The Musical* by 2008. But she was not there for long. Next stop, Hollywood.

Ice Queen

One of Ariana's earliest performances (billed as "Ariana Grande-Butera") was the singing of 'Star-Spangled Banner' before a Florida Panthers ice hockey match – broadcast live on Fox Sports Net. The video, still available on YouTube, demonstrates one of the earliest examples of the singer's superb talent. Perfectly in tune, perfectly dressed and perfectly performed, young Ariana shows what she becomes famous for years later. She is well-rehearsed and a stunning performer, it is hard to believe she is only 8 years old. Years later, she described it as "My first big gig" on *The Tonight Show* with Jimmy Fallon.

TV Calling

The budding actress and singer did not have to wait long before she landed a role on the small screen. Nickelodeon channel came calling, with a supporting role on the show *Victorious*, a musical sitcom (a song every few episodes) that originally ran for four seasons from 2010. Grande played the part of Cat Valentine (central character Tori's "strange" friend who has red hair and is vegan), and the show went down well with fans despite a lack of critical appreciation.

Victorious spawned toys, dolls, a videogame (chart-topping, Ariana Grande-featuring) soundtracks, awards (2012 Kids' Choice Award for Favorite TV Show) and then a spin-off, *Sam & Cat*, which put Ariana in the spotlight.

Fame

Following a few setbacks, including how the bleaching and dying of her hair to play Cat "completely destroyed my hair" as Grande said on Facebook, and although it had high ratings, *Sam & Cat* only ran one 35-episode season. It did pick up a few awards, but it was not renewed. However, Grande was on the road to fame. All this performing was enabling the already determined and talented actress to practise and perfect her art. And her chosen art was singing. Despite already being a truly brilliant performer (a "triple-threat" as those able to sing, dance and act are known), Grande wanted to be a singer so that's the area she pursued, in her typical hardworking and lazer-focused fashion.

" I started tweeting when
I was 13. I thought it
was a great way to keep
in touch with people
I knew. And I always
thought that social
media was a great way
to save memories. "

Interview with Anne Geggis,
Sun Sentinel, 31 August 2012

Chapter Two

Inspiration, Image, Impact

Voice Coach Vetro

While filming *Victorious* and *Sam & Cat*, Grande was singing as much as she could. She sang on the show, but was also doing plenty on her own and with help, notably from the vocal coach Eric Vetro (who Grande was working with before she landed her role in *13: The Musical*). Vetro has a truly star-studded client list, which includes John Legend, Shawn Mendes, Pink, Camila Cabello and Katy Perry.

In 2021, Grande called Vetro "My friend and vocal coach of over 13 years" in an Instagram post, saying "he has been by my side every step of the way and believed in and encouraged me." The practise would not go to waste.

Four Octave Range

The key to Ariana's vocal performances is how easily she seems to reach the top end of her – very impressive – four-octave range. Although she does not have the breath control of a classical soprano, she never throws a breath away, using it instead to communicate emotion and add texture to her sound. She easily switches from softly vocalized mid-range to a characteristic belt – a mix of chest and head voice.

Whistle Register

While her speaking voice oscillates between a high pitch and a lower, raspier register, her singing voice attains earth-shattering high notes known as the whistle register. Belting in the whistle register requires little air, as the vocal chords are tightened, so you don't have to take a deep breath before sustaining a note. This is why Ariana Grande can hold a whistle note for up to 15 seconds!

Melisma:
Also called a roulade,
this is defined as singing
a single syllable of text
while moving between
different notes in
succession.

Ariana has a unique way
of achieving this effect –
by wobbling her jaw.

YouTube Generation

What did any young, aspiring musical artist do in the 2000s? Put videos of themselves singing on YouTube of course. To say it worked for Justin Bieber and others would be an understatement. So Ariana Grande followed that well-trodden path, uploading a number of homemade videos, including covers of Rihanna's 'Love the Way You Lie', Bruno Mars' 'Grenade', racking up millions of views. The latter ending 2010 in YouTube's No. 1 spot, having blasted its way up the charts.

As of 2024, Ariana Grande had 54 million subscribers on YouTube. Her channel was first known as osnapitzari, which means "Oh snap, it's Ari", a reference to the Disney series *That's So Raven*.

Signing

Her YouTube cover numbers, combined with her obvious talent and propensity for hard work – it was obvious that she was a rounded performer even at that stage – meant that it was not long before the young singer came to the attention of some of the big names in the music business.

By 2011 she was signed to Universal Republic, with the label's President and CEO Monte Lipman making the following statement: "We're thrilled to have her join Universal Republic." It is unlikely that Lipman realized back then just how thrilled they would be later when the young woman's career sent her to the top of multiple charts all over the world.

Put Your Hearts Up

The label wasted no time in getting a first single out. However, it was not one to remember, and Grande herself made it clear that she regretted the single and its release, telling *Rolling Stone* later that, "It was geared toward kids and felt so inauthentic and fake. That was the worst moment of my life." The single was born from her desire to dive straight into the music industry, and the label's desire to draw on her Nickelodeon fanbase. The track did admittedly go gold, but to say Grande is not proud of it would be a serious understatement.

A Learning Process

Throughout her career, Ariana Grande has demonstrated that she is intelligent, that she can learn from perceived mistakes and – crucially – that when she is honest and believes in herself, she makes her best work. The 'Put Your Hearts Up' fiasco was a prime example, and by the time her debut album was released in 2013, the singer was singing and performing much closer to what she felt was right. And the extent to which that decision was justified is clearly shown in terms of album sales and critical acknowledgement.

Yours Truly hit the ground running and it debuted on the top spot of the Billboard chart in the USA, and was a Top 10 starter in the UK, Australia and the Netherlands.

First Album

Yours Truly was a largely pop and R&B album, with 12 carefully produced tracks featuring numerous collaborators, including Big Sean, Mac Miller, Mika and Nathan Sykes of The Wanted. There were a few special editions, for example, the iTunes special edition with an extra version of 'The Way' ('Spanglish', featuring Mac Miller) and two Japanese editions with extra tracks. The album, which had been recorded over a two-year period, went platinum in the USA.

'Put Your Hearts Up' was originally meant to be the first single from the album, but the album's direction was reassessed, and the resulting album is very different.

Yours Truly
Five Fun Facts

1 The Japanese release of the album featured a different cover image with Ariana in close-up.

2 Lead track 'The Way' samples the 1998 Big Pun song 'Still Not a Prayer'.

3 Many tracks didn't make it to the album, including 'La Vie En Rose' and 'Pink Champagne'.

4 The original album cover was pink and featured an image of Grande in lingerie. It was dropped.

5 Ariana listed the following as her major influences on the album: Amy Winehouse, Mariah Carey, Whitney Houston, Alicia Keys, Fergie, Katy Perry and Madonna.

"I would write songs about what was happening in my life. So it's really personal."

Ariana Grande on *Yours Truly*, SheKnows, 2013

Yours Truly

1. 'Honeymoon Avenue'
2. 'Baby I'
3. 'Right There' (feat. Big Sean)
4. 'Tattooed Heart'
5. 'Lovin' It'
6. 'Piano'
7. 'Daydreamin''
8. 'The Way' (feat. Mac Miller)
9. 'You'll Never Know'
10. 'Almost Is Never Enough' (with Nathan Sykes)
11. 'Popular Song' (Mika feat. Ariana Grande)
12. 'Better Left Unsaid'

It's Christmas Time

Ariana Grande has recorded a number of Christmas songs, starting in 2013 with the *Christmas Kisses* EP. The songs were first released one by one over a five-week period, starting with her cover of Wham's 'Last Christmas'. Then she released – in order – 'Love Is Everything', 'Snow in California' and 'Santa Baby' (featuring Elizabeth Gillies, her fellow actor from *Victorious*). In a tweet, Grande revealed that 'Santa Baby' was her favourite.

Two years later, in 2015, she released *Christmas & Chill*, another themed EP, this time with six original tracks all co-written by Grande herself.

Naughty Santa

There is a bonus track hidden in some editions of this release. Named 'Santa Tell Me' (Naughty Version), it has lyrics that are a little more explicit than the original.

Performing for the President

In March 2014, Ariana Grande sang at the concert Women of Soul: In Performance at the White House. She performed a cover version of Whitney Houston's 'I Have Nothing' and her own 'Tattooed Heart'. The young singer was one of few chosen for the event by First Lady Michelle Obama, joining female singing royalty such as Patti LaBelle, Janelle Monae, Jill Scott, Tessanne Chin, and queen of soul Aretha Franklin.

When she stood to sing her first song, Grande greeted the President and the First Lady in a rather non-traditional manner, saying "What's up? How are ya?" This cheeky start elicited laughter, but the audience was very much concentrated on the quality of her singing when her performance began.

Two for Gold

Fans did not have to wait long for Grande's second album. One year after *Yours Truly*, almost to the day, *My Everything* was released on 22 August 2014. Although the sound of the album was more mature than her debut, the album still hit the apex of the Billboard Hot Top 100, and was a Top 10 charting album in territories all around the world.

Once again Grande worked with a wide array of talented writers, performers and producers, and this was reflected in the critical acclaim the record received, building on her debut.

Five singles were released from *My Everything*, and each one performed well. It was just the start of Grande's huge recording successes.

There are many guest appearances on *My Everything*. Three of the best tracks must be:

1 'Break Your Heart Right Back'
– Childish Gambino

2 'Problem' – Iggy Azalea

3 'Bang Bang' – Jessie J and Nicki Minaj
(deluxe edition only)

"I sang it about my personal things that are holding me back, my fears, certain negativities in my life ... Things I was afraid of."

Ariana Grande on 'Break Free', *Time*, 2014

"I had to stand on a box for our shots together. I [was] like, 'I need a ladder over here.'"

Ariana Grande on making a video with Iggy Azalea, *Time*, 2014

My Everything

1. 'Intro'
2. 'Problem' (feat. Iggy Azalea)
3. 'One Last Time'
4. 'Why Try'
5. 'Break Free' (feat. Zedd)
6. 'Best Mistake' (feat. Big Sean)
7. 'Be My Baby' (feat. Cashmere Cat)
8. 'Break Your Heart Right Back'
(feat. Childish Gambino)
9. 'Love Me Harder' (with the Weeknd)
10. 'Just a Little Bit of Your Heart'
11. 'Hands on Me' (feat. ASAP Ferg)
12. 'My Everything'

"My brother was always the one in the spotlight and I liked that."

Ariana Grande, *Billboard*, 2014

Big Brother

Frankie James Grande may "only" be Ariana's half-brother, but the two are very close. Frankie has had his (unfortunately well-publicized) demons, but his little sister has always been there, supporting however she can. He's a self-confessed nerd too, stating on Instagram after he was married to Hale Leon: "Hale and I were married at a small intimate galactic ceremony in my family home in Florida on May the 4th Be with You [Star Wars Day], cause we really are both that nerdy."

Frankie works on Broadway, acting in his own shows and others, as well as producing.

Grande Collaborations: Mac Miller

At first the relationship between Mac and Ariana was strictly professional, but in 2016 the two began dating, and they recorded together various times. Two years later they were no longer an item – Ariana was engaged to comedian Pete Davidson – when the news came through that Miller had taken an accidental overdose and died.

The loss hit Grande hard, much of it revealed on social media, including a post that included the sentences, "you were my dearest friend. for so long. above anything else. i'm so sorry i couldn't fix or take your pain away. i really wanted to."

"I engineered the session. I recorded him rapping, while I was simultaneously baking cookies for him and that was that."

Ariana Grande on Mac Miller, and recording 'The Way', *Rolling Stone*, 2013

"It really
does feel like
a girl group
moment."

Mariah Carey on recording 'Oh Santa!'
with Jennifer Hudson and Ariana Grande,
Billboard, 2020

Grande Collaborations:
Mariah Carey & Jennifer Hudson

When three female legends of pop united for a new version of an old song – 'Oh Santa!' (on the tenth anniversary no less) – it could have gone horribly wrong. But it didn't – it created an entirely new, awesome audio experience. Teaming up with Mariah and Jennifer may have been daunting for Ariana, but she brings so much to the table that everybody wins.

When asked by *Complex* about being compared to Mariah in 2013, Grande responded in her trademark mature fashion: "If I complained about being compared to the greatest vocalist who ever lived, I would be a very dumb, ungrateful person... It's a massive compliment."

Ariana Grande

Ariana on Tour:
The Listening Sessions

Grande embarked on her first headlining concert
tour in 2013, in support of *Yours Truly*. It was a
restrained affair with 11 nights in the US and
Canada across August and September in small,
intimate venues – but any fans lucky enough to
get tickets were not complaining, as music from
the as-yet-unreleased album was played.

Set list

1. 'Baby I'

2. 'Lovin' It'

3. 'You'll Never Know'

4. 'Honeymoon Avenue'

5. 'Tattooed Heart'

6. 'Better Left Unsaid'

7. 'Daydreamin''

8. 'Almost Is Never Enough'

9. 'Piano'

10. 'Right There'

11. 'The Way'

Ariana on Tour:
The Honeymoon

Grande's second foray on the road was a much grander affair than her first: this was global. In support of *My Everything*, Ariana embarked on a tour that lasted nearly the whole of 2015, starting at the Independence Events Center in Independence, Missouri, on 25 February and ending in the Allianz Parque in São Paulo, Brazil on 25 October. She passed through North America, Europe, Japan, the Philippines, Indonesia and South America.

The Honeymoon Tour

88 shows across 4 continents

Guest appearances from Big Sean
(1) and Justin Bieber (2)

The stage had 3 levels
and a catwalk

20 songs in the set, divided
up into 8 acts

Chapter Three
Growth & Transformation

The Third Album

In May of 2016, Grande released her third album, *Dangerous Woman*. She had been working on songs since the release of *My Everything*, even while on an extended world tour.

At first, there was some fan (and industry) confusion about the title, as it was originally named *Moonlight*, learned after Grande's response to a fan on Twitter, but that was changed to *Dangerous Woman*, because Grande saw that as more empowering.

"A dangerous woman is someone who's not afraid to take a stand, be herself and to be honest."

Ariana Grande on the title of her third album,
Billboard, 2016

Great Team

For *Dangerous Woman*, Grande worked with
various producers, including Max Martin
with whom she had collaborated on *My
Everything*. She said of Martin, "He's like a
mathematician. He knows music like math.
It just makes sense to him."

The usual high-quality collaborations were
present, this time including Nicki Minaj,
Macy Gray, Lil Wayne and Future.

Dangerous Woman

1. 'Moonlight'
2. 'Dangerous Woman'
3. 'Be Alright'
4. 'Into You'
5. 'Side to Side' (feat. Nicki Minaj)
6. 'Let Me Love You' (feat. Lil Wayne)
7. 'Greedy'
8. 'Leave Me Lonely' (feat. Macy Gray)
9. 'Everyday' (feat. Future)
10. 'Bad Decisions'
11. 'Thinking Bout You'

An Important Step

Dangerous Woman was another critical success for Grande, with most pundits acknowledging the skill, effort and talent that had obviously gone into the recording process.

Curiously, *Dangerous Woman* was Grande's only album that did not debut on the top position of the Billboard 200, "only" reaching No. 2. However, it did eventually go double platinum in the USA, heading towards the half-million mark. The album fared extremely well across the world, hitting the top spot in various countries.

"I want to be empowering my fans. I feel like my personal growth is reflected in the sound."

Ariana Grande on *Dangerous Woman*, *Billboard*, 2016

Dangerous Woman was nominated
for the Best Pop Vocal Album and
Grande nominated for the Best Pop
Solo Performance at the Grammy
Awards in 2017 but she lost out to
Adele both times.

However, the album did win
International Album of the Year
at the Japan Gold Disc Awards,
highlighting the artist's phenomenal
popularity in that country.

Three Times A Lady

When the single 'Dangerous Woman' was released, it hit the Top 10 in the Billboard Hot 100 and made Ariana Grande the first artist with debut singles from their first three albums to hit those heights. And when 'No Tears Left to Cry' from *Sweetener* also debuted in the Top 10, she set another record!

Record Breaker

Ariana is in the unique position of being the holder of 20 Guinness World Records. One of the best is her record for the most songs (6) to debut at No. 1 on the Billboard 200 chart. Taylor Swift is the only one to match that feat.

Grande's records – three more reasons Ariana is the best:

1 Most streamed track on Spotify in one week (female): 71 million.

2 First female artist to replace herself at No. 1 on the UK singles chart (first time ever).

3 First solo artist to occupy positions 1, 2 and 3 simultaneously on US singles chart.

Queen of the Screen

It seems like ages ago that we saw a young Ariana on Nickelodeon shows. She has made many appearances since then, primarily as an interviewee on pretty much every decent chat show (always a great guest: polite, funny, knowledgeable, humble), but she's also turned up in many other interesting shows, from *Scream Queens* and *Hairspray Live!* to 'Carpool Karaoke' and the movie *Don't Look Up*. Nobody is quite sure how she finds the time to put in such well-rounded performances on a regular basis, but she does it!

No Kidding!

Grande made a cameo appearance in 2018 on Jim Carrey's comedy *Kidding*, when she played the part of Piccola Grande, the Pickle Fairy of Hope.

Ariana on Tour: Dangerous Woman

Following Grande's continuing musical successes and the Honeymoon Tour, the singer took to the road in 2017 on the Dangerous Woman Tour. It was another truly global event, starting in Phoenix, Arizona, in February 2017 and ending in Hong Kong on 21 September. Reflecting the maturity of her sound, Grande's costumes for the tour were revised and re-thought. According to Bryan Hearns, the costume developer for the tour, the look was "confident, feminine and dangerous".

Dangerous
Woman Tour

77 shows across 5 continents

Guest appearances from Victoria Monét, BIA, Jason Robert Brown and Mac Miller

12 dates cancelled, for various reasons

Tragedy

During the tour, as the crowds left after Grande's concert in Manchester, UK, on 17 May 2017, a suicide bomber detonated a device, killing 22 people. This became known as the Manchester Arena Bombing and it had a profound effect on the artist, but instead of simply moving on and continuing her tour, she bravely decided to return to Manchester. She admitted to having dizzy spells afterwards, and increased anxiety. She subsequently wrote the song 'Get Well Soon' with Pharrell Williams for the album *Sweetener*.

"It's not my trauma. It's those families. It's their losses, and so it's hard to just let it all out without thinking about them reading this and reopening the memory for them."

Ariana on the Manchester Arena Bombing, *Vogue*, 2019

One Love Manchester, 4 June 2017

Following the bombing, Grande cancelled her remaining tour dates until 5 June and immediately turned her attention to organizing a benefit concert for the victims and families of the bombing. The show was called One Love Manchester and it took place only 13 days after the attack, on the cricket ground at Old Trafford, Manchester.

A host of stars stepped
in to perform, from
Ariana Grande herself to
Coldplay, and including
such pop royalty as Justin
Bieber, Pharrell Williams,
the Black Eyed Peas and
Katy Perry. An enormous
success, the event raised
more than £17 million
($21 million) for the cause.

One Love Grande

Ariana Grande fans who had been present at her original concert were invited for free, trams were run at no charge, and Uber donated their fares to the charity. Tickets for One Love Manchester were cheaply priced and subject to no booking fees; the event sold out in minutes.

Ariana Grande opened and closed the concert, finishing with an extremely emotional rendition of 'Somewhere Over the Rainbow' and the event was broadcast live on television and radio around the world.

*

Ariana Grande was made an "Honorary Citizen" by the City of Manchester. It was the first time this had been bestowed on someone.

"She's like an R-rated version of a Disney character, super-vivid."

Pharrell Williams on Ariana Grande, *Vogue*, 2019

Onwards Ariana

Ariana Grande channelled her emotion and in August 2018, her fourth album, *Sweetener*, was released. Half of the album was produced by Grande's usual collaborators, including Max Martin, but many tracks were produced by the legendary Pharrell Williams. The record, which earned Grande her first Grammy Award (Best Pop Vocal Album) is acknowledged as a step up in terms of musical and lyrical maturity.

It went straight to the No. 1 spot on the Billboard 200, giving Grande a hat-trick. It topped charts around the world, and the single 'No Tears Left to Cry', written in the wake of the Manchester Arena Bombing was a huge bestseller too.

Sweetener

1. 'Raindrops (An Angel Cried)'
2. 'Blazed' (feat. Pharrell Williams)
3. 'The Light Is Coming' (feat. Nicki Minaj)
4. 'R.E.M'.
5. 'God Is a Woman'
6. 'Sweetener'
7. 'Successful'
8. 'Everytime'
9. 'Breathin''
10. 'No Tears Left to Cry'
11. 'Borderline' (feat. Missy Elliott)
12. 'Better Off'
13. 'Goodnight N Go'
14. 'Pete Davidson'
15. 'Get Well Soon'

"I want it to be positive and talk about positivity and love. I don't have any tears left to cry."

Producer Savan Kotecha reveals Ariana Grande's wishes for 'No Tears Left to Cry', *Billboard*, 2018

Ariana Grande

Sweetener World Tour

100 shows

1,300,000 attendees

$146,000,000 box office

2 nights as part of the Coachella festival

Guest appearances by Justin Bieber, Victoria Monét, NSYNC and Nicky Minaj

Costumes by Versace and Michael Ngo

On the Road

To promote *Sweetener*, Grande performed
four nights (three in the USA, one in London,
England) in small venues. Billed as the
Sweetener Sessions, some nights she played
more than 20 songs.

This was only a warm-up for the Sweetener
World Tour, which kicked off in March 2019 and
continued until the end of the year. It was her
biggest tour to date and cemented her status as
a world player in pop performance.

Work, Work, Work

Not one to rest on her laurels, Grande was ready to release her fifth album in February 2019. Always writing, always working, it was only six months after *Sweetener*, and coincided with the previous album's world tour!

Thank U, Next was an even more personal work, and dealt with some of Grande's personal issues, including grief and empowerment. The singles '7 Rings' and 'Thank U, Next' came out first and were both huge, contributing to the album's success with critics and fans alike. And sales were stellar, with more records broken, as the top three slots of the Billboard chart were taken up with songs from the album.

Smashing the Charts

When Ariana Grande occupied the top three positions on the Billboard Hot 100 in February 2019, she became the first female artist ever to achieve this. The songs were 'Thank U, Next', '7 Rings' and 'Break Up with Your Girlfriend, I'm Bored'.

Thank U, Next
Five Facts

1 None of the tracks credit other artists, unlike all previous albums.

2 '7 Rings' features samples from 'My Favorite Things' by Rodgers & Hammerstein.

3 Physical and digital album versions have different cover art.

4 Every track on the album was co-written by Ariana.

5 A fragrance, Thank U, Next, was also released by Grande.

Thank U, Next

1. 'Imagine'
2. 'Needy'
3. 'NASA'
4. 'Bloodline'
5. 'Fake Smile'
6. 'Bad Idea'
7. 'Make Up'
8. 'Ghostin''
9. 'In My Head'
10. '7 Rings'
11. 'Thank U, Next'
12. 'Break Up with Your Girlfriend, I'm Bored'

Award Wins

2014 **MTV Video Music Awards for Best Pop Video**
– 'Problem' (feat. Iggy Azalea)

2017 **2017FiFi Awards Fragrance of the Year for Women's Popular** – Sweet Like Candy

2018 **MTV Video Music Awards for Best Pop Video**
– 'No Tears Left to Cry'

2019 **MTV Video Music Awards for Best Art Direction**
– '7 Rings'

MTV Video Music Awards for Artist of the Year

FiFi Awards Fragrance of the Year for Women's Popular – Cloud

Billboard Music Awards for Top Female Artist

Billboard Chart Achievement Award

BRIT Award for International Female Solo Artist

Grammy Award for Best Pop Vocal Album
– *Sweetener*

MTV Video Music Awards for Song of the Year
– 'Rain on Me' (with Lady Gaga)

2021 **Grammy Award for Best Pop Duo/Group Performance** – 'Rain on Me' (with Lady Gaga)

"I have to be the luckiest girl in the world, and the unluckiest, for sure."

Ariana Grande interview with Rob Haskell
in *Vogue*, 2019

Ariana Grande

Grande
Abbreviations

ME *My Everything*

DW *Dangerous Woman*

SW/SWT *Sweetener*

TUN *Thank U, Next*

PST/POS *Positions*

ES *Eternal Sunshine*

Thank U Very Much

'Thank U, Next' was the most-watched music video on YouTube within 24 hours of release, the fastest video on Vivo to reach 100 million streams and was the most streamed song by a female artist over a 24-hour time frame... Until Ariana broke that record with '7 Rings'.

"I made it with my best friends over a small period of time and it kind of, like, saved my life..."

Ariana Grande on making the album
Thank U, Next, Zach Sang Show, 2019

" It's fun, it's pop music, and I'm not trying to make it sound like anything that it's not, but these songs to me really do represent some heavy shit. "

Ariana Grande on getting personal in
Thank U, Next, Vogue, 2019

Grande Collaborations: Iggy Azalea

Possibly the highlight of *My Everything*, the catchy, multilayered song 'Problem' was a hit around the world. The track won Best Pop Video at the 2014 MTV Europe Music Awards, testament to the all-round high quality of the writing, producing and performing of this now-classic song.

*

Three Times Over

Adele was the first female artist to have three Top 10 singles (as a lead). The second was Ariana Grande in 2014, with 'Problem', 'Break Free' and 'Bang Bang'.

By the end of 2020, Ariana was ready to release her next album: *Positions*. It continues with intimate themes, as in her previous efforts, and although similar in style, it highlights the singer's amazing vocal talent even more. Ariana again co-wrote all of the songs, and this time returned with a number of collaborations. *Positions* became Grande's fifth No. 1 album in the USA, and it performed really well around the world.

In *Positions*, Grande answers her critics, gets a bit steamy with some adult content, but above all sings her heart out; again the record was critically acclaimed and the songs were snapped up by fans in big numbers on streaming services.

Positions

1. 'Shut Up'
2. '34+35'
3. 'Motive' (with Doja Cat)
4. 'Just Like Magic'
5. 'Off the Table' (with the Weeknd)
6. 'Six Thirty'
7. 'Safety Net' (featuring Ty Dolla $ign)
8. 'My Hair'
9. 'Nasty'
10. 'West Side'
11. 'Love Language'
12. 'Positions'
13. 'Obvious'
14. 'POV'

An extra five tracks grace the deluxe edition of the album:
1. 'Someone Like U' (interlude) **2.** 'Test Drive' **3.** '34+35'
(remix, featuring Doja Cat and Megan Thee Stallion)
4. 'Worst Behavior' **5.** 'Main Thing'

Surprise Swim

At the 2020 Adult Swim Festival, fans of Thundercat found themselves in for a rare treat when Ariana Grande took to the stage (the *Aqua Teen Hunger Force* kitchen to be precise) unannounced to perform the song 'Them Changes'. Grande had played the song before, notably at the BBC Radio 1 Live Lounge session two years previously, even referring to the track as one of her favourites.

Concert Movie

The Sweetener World Tour was such a major event that it was only fair that everyone could get the chance to see it. And sure enough, in December 2020, Netflix exclusively released *Ariana Grande: Excuse Me, I Love You* on the small screen. It came out approximately one year after the tour ended, and the feature-length movie featured Grande performing 25 songs, as well as some behind-the-scenes content of the superstar and her entourage.

The majority of the live footage was from the concert in the O2 Arena in London.

Grande's first live album, *K Bye for Now (SWT Live)* contained music from the same tour, and had been released in December 2019, as the tour ended.

Chapter Four
Ariana Now!

Wait For Me

Fans expecting another Ariana Grande album
quickly were in for a disappointment. It was
to be a four-year gap between releases – the
longest in any point of her career. But in 2024,
the seventh album in Grande's amazing career
was announced and then released. *Eternal
Sunshine* marked a significant step in the
evolution of an artist who has remained the
same – honest, open, truthful – while almost
constantly evolving in terms of maturity of
music and lyrical prowess.

\\ ... the loss and grief that you hear on the album, some of the heartbreak stuff, there was so much love and transparency. That was something I really wanted to make sure was captured. \\

Ariana Grande on *Eternal Sunshine*, *Zach Sang Show*, February 2024

Back to Work

Back with Max Martin and Ilya Salmanzadeh
co-producing most tracks, Ariana herself wrote
the lyrics, music and (co-) produced all the
songs on the album. Working with a smaller
team than usual, the album has a pared-down
feel and, despite her usual pop and R&B sound,
includes other diverse influences, including
more synthesizer and guitar- and string-based
tracks. As you would expect, the album hit
the top spot in the US Billboard charts as well
as other territories around the world: another
triumph for the artist.

Eternal Sunshine

1. 'Intro (End of the World)'
2. 'Bye'
3. 'Don't Wanna Break Up Again'
4. 'Saturn Returns Interlude'
5. 'Eternal Sunshine'
6. 'Supernatural'
7. 'True Story'
8. 'The Boy Is Mine'
9. 'Yes, And?'
10. 'We Can't Be Friends (Wait for Your Love)'
11. 'I Wish I Hated You'
12. 'Imperfect for You'
13. 'Ordinary Things' (feat. Nonna*)

* Yes, Ariana's grandma!

Ariana Grande

Charity Work

Ariana has long been an advocate for good causes, and even helped to found a charity when she was only 10 years old. Since then she has gone on to raise tens of millions of dollars for a variety of good causes.

She has donated, played benefit concerts for, and helped to publicize many charities, including Planned Parenthood, LGBTQ+ causes, gun control, homeless youth, cancer and more.

Her biggest single endeavour came at the One Love Manchester concert that she organized and performed at after the horrific attack following he Manchester concert during her Dangerous Woman Tour. She has donated the proceeds of many of her recordings to charity.

"Therapy should not be for a privileged few but something everyone has access to."

Ariana Grande, Instagram, 2021

Business Is Business

Ariana Grande is so much more than a singer. As would be expected with a mother who was CEO of a company, she is very astute and as good at making money as she is at giving it away (see page 118). Her business empire is big and growing, stretching across various categories, notably fragrances and beauty.

Her first fragrance, Ari by Ariana Grande, came out in 2015 and since then she has released another five, all of which have been very well received, including prizes at the annual FiFi Awards ceremonies (like the Oscars for scent). She has sold more than $1 billion worth of perfume across the world: smells like success!

Grande's r.e.m. beauty line is also a fantastic success, and features makeup, skincare and other beauty products.

Grande Style

Ariana has always been about the sound: her voice and the music she creates. But she is without a doubt a major style icon of the 21st century, particularly for young women around the world. She has been on the cover of *Vogue* (US, British and *Teen*), *Cosmopolitan*, *Time*, *Marie Claire*, *Seventeen*, *Elle* and pretty much every entertainment magazine that's worth a read. Fashion designers love to dress her, and her concerts are colourful, classy affairs that celebrate femininity and power.

"I don't want people to talk about my choices or how little I'm wearing. I just want the conversation to be about the music and what I'm creating. "

Ariana on what is important to her,
Complex, 5 November 2013

Follow Me:
Ariana Grande has more than 380 million Instagram followers, putting her firmly in the global Top 10 (6, actually).

Big Numbers:
Ariana Grande has more than 98 billion streams so far, making her one of the most listened to artists of all time.

Arianators

Ariana Grande has a lot of fans. A LOT of fans. Her tracks sell in huge numbers, her tours sell out and all her business ventures turn to gold (pretty quickly!). The hard work she puts in is reflected swiftly. And that is also true of her huge army of fans, the Arianators. She frequently engages with her fanbase and is hugely appreciative of them, loving the support they give her. She has always given a lot of herself on social media and in her music: long may it continue.

Social Media

"I've been open in my art and open in my DMs and my conversations with my fans directly, and I want to be there for them, so I share things that I think they'll find comfort in knowing that I go through as well..."

Ariana Grande interview with Rob Haskell in *Vogue*, 9 July 2019

✳

Keep on Breakin'

When '7 Rings' was released it became Spotify's most popular debut of all time, with 14.9 million listens in its first 24 hours. She later broke the record with 'Stuck with U' and 'Rain on Me' (with Lady Gaga).

Fab Three

The last artist to occupy the Billboard Hot 100 top three positions before Ariana Grande? The Beatles... in 1964.

"I don't feel much pressure to fit in. I never have. I've always just wanted to do my thing."

Ariana Grande on industry pressure to change, *Rolling Stone*, 2013